**SCIENCE ANSWERS**

# Food Chains and Webs

## FROM PRODUCERS TO DECOMPOSERS

Heinemann Library
Chicago, Illinois

**Louise and Richard Spilsbury**

Design: Richard Parker and Celia Floyd
Illustrations: John Fleck/Heinemann
  Library
Picture Research: Rebecca Sodergren
  and Pete Morris
Originated by Dot Gradations Ltd.
Printed in China by WKT
  Company Limited

08 07 06 05
10 9 8 7 6 5 4 3 2

**Library of Congress Cataloging-in-Publication Data**
Spilsbury, Louise.
  Food chains and webs : from producers to
decomposers / Louise Spilsbury and
Richard Spilsbury.
      v. cm. -- (Science answers)
  Includes bibliographical references and
index.
  Contents: What are food chains and
webs? -- What types of food webs are found
in grasslands? -- Who eats whom in oceans,
rivers and lakes? -- What are the food webs
in deserts? -- Who eats whom in forests? --
What are the food webs in towns and
cities? -- People who found the answers --
Amazing facts.
  ISBN 1-4034-4764-0 (lib. bdg.) -- ISBN 1-
4034-5510-4 (pbk.)
  1.  Food chains (Ecology)--Juvenile
literature. [1. Food chains (Ecology) 2.
Ecology.]  I. Spilsbury, Richard, 1963- II.
Title. III. Series.
  QH541.14.S68 2004
  577'.16--dc22

                           2003025660

**Acknowledgments**
The author and publishers are grateful to
the following for permission to reproduce
copyright material:

p.5 Guy Edwards/NHPA; p.6 Digital
Vision/Getty Images; p.7 Fritz
Polking/FLPA; pp.8, 9 Minden
Pictures/FLPA; p.11 Image Quest 3D/NHPA;
pp.12, 14 Oxford Scientific Films; p.13
Norbert Wu/NHPA; p.15 Bill Coster/NHPA;
pp.16, 27 Tudor Photography/Harcourt
Education Ltd.; p.17 Daniel Heuclin/NHPA;
p.18 Wendy Dennis/FLPA; p.19 Hellio &
Van Ingen/NHPA; pp.21, 25 Stephen
Dalton/NHPA; p.22 B. & C.
Alexander/NHPA; p.23 Jany
Sauvanet/NHPA; p.26 Steve
Maslowski/FLPA; p.28 Bettmann/Corbis;
p.29 Photodisc/Getty.

Cover photograph reproduced with
permission of Fritz Polking/FLPA.

Every effort has been made to contact
copyright holders of any material
reproduced in this book. Any omissions
will be rectified in subsequent printings
if notice is given to the publisher.

Some words are shown in
bold, **like this.** You can find
out what they mean by
looking in the glossary.

# Contents

## About the activities

This book contains some sections called Science Answers. Each one describes an activity that you can try yourself. By doing them you will get a chance to research and make your own food chains and webs. You will find out more about the feeding relationships in a variety of **habitats.**

## Materials you will use

Most of the activities in this book can be done with objects that you can find in your own home. You will also need a pencil and paper to record your results.

# What Are Food Chains and Webs?

Food chains and food webs are diagrams that show a series of living things that eat each other to get energy. All plants and animals need energy to live. The Sun is the source of all energy on Earth. Plants trap this energy to make their own food. Animals get energy by eating plants or other animals.

### Plants and animals linked together

Every living thing is like a link in a food chain. The first link in a chain could be a leaf on a plant. Then a slug eats the leaf. A toad eats the slug. In this way, energy is passed from one link to the next.

### Food chains put together

Most animals eat more than one kind of food. This means that they are part of two or more food chains. The different food chains connect with each other to form food webs.

## How are food chains and webs different?

A food chain follows a simple line, like a chain. For example, berries are eaten by voles, which are eaten by lynx. Food chains join together to form a more complicated pattern that looks like a spider's web. Note that in this food web an arrow is drawn from each **organism** pointing to the organism that eats it.

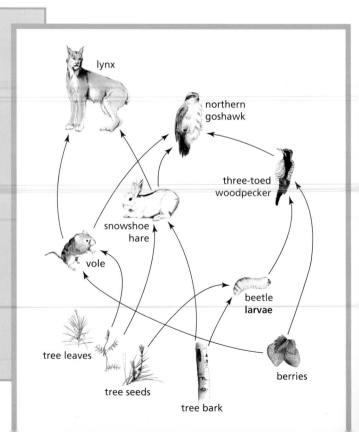

lynx

northern goshawk

three-toed woodpecker

snowshoe hare

vole

beetle larvae

tree leaves

tree seeds

tree bark

berries

## The beginning of food chains and food webs

All food chains and food webs start with plants. Plants trap the Sun's energy in their leaves. They use this energy to combine water and **carbon dioxide** to make food in the form of sugars. This process is called **photosynthesis.** Plants are known as **producers** because they produce food.

### How do leaves trap energy?

Plant leaves use the energy in sunlight to make food. They use a substance called chlorophyll to trap the energy. Chlorophyll gives the leaves their green color.

Animals are **consumers.** Some animals eat plants to get the energy stored inside the plants. These animals are called **herbivores.** They feed on plant parts such as leaves, seeds, berries, or nuts. Other animals eat the herbivores. These animals are called **carnivores. Omnivores** are animals that eat both plants and animals. When animals die, **scavengers** and **decomposers** eat their remains and break them down to get energy.

## Primary and secondary consumers

Plants produce food for themselves, but animals take advantage of this food supply by eating the plants. **Herbivores** are called primary **consumers** because they are the first animals to eat plants. They are the first to consume some of this energy. Secondary consumers are animals that eat primary consumers. **Carnivores, scavengers,** and **decomposers** are all secondary consumers. **Omnivores** are both primary and secondary consumers because they eat both plants and other plant-eating animals.

## Decomposers and energy recycling

When a plant or animal dies, the energy in its body is not wasted. Decomposers such as **fungi** and **bacteria** feed on the remains of living things. Decomposers break plants and animals down into **nutrients,** some of which they use and some of which get washed into the soil. Plants take in some of these nutrients from the soil when they take in water through their roots. Plants use the recycled nutrients to grow.

### Fruit fans

This orangutan is a primary consumer. It is a herbivore that eats plant parts that it finds in the forests of Southeast Asia. Its favorite meal is fruit.

## How many links do food chains have?

The number of links in a single food chain is usually only four or five. Each living thing in the chain uses up some energy to grow and move. Energy is continually being lost as it is passed along the food chain. This is why food webs always have more **producers** than primary consumers, and more primary consumers than secondary consumers. For example, in the African savanna there are more grass plants than there are zebras that eat them. There are more zebras than there are lions.

## Habitats and food chains

A place where an animal or plant lives is called its **habitat.** Each habitat contains different **organisms** that are adapted to live there. In this book you will look at different kinds of habitats and the food chains and webs that exist within them.

# What Kinds of Food Webs Are Found in Grasslands?

In grasslands the soil is too poor or the weather is too dry for trees and many other plants to grow. Only tough grasses can grow here. They form the basis of grassland food chains.

One kind of grassland is called a savanna. Savannas have scattered trees and shrubs. But most of a savanna is covered with grass. Some savannas grow in **tropical** places, while others grow in areas with hot summers and cold winters. Another kind of grassland has even fewer trees and shrubs. It is almost entirely covered in grasses. These are called prairies in the United States, pampas in Argentina, and steppe in Asia.

### Primary consumers

Small and large **herbivores** graze on the different kinds of grasses in the world's grasslands. Many butterflies, bees, and other insects feed on **nectar** from flowers. Caterpillars, beetles, and grasshoppers munch the leaves.

### Ants and anteaters

Giant anteaters like this one are about the size of large dogs. They eat up to 30,000 grassland ants and termites a day, catching them with their long, sticky tongues. The insects are primary consumers that feed on grassland plants.

Many grassland herbivores are **rodents** with sharp front teeth for gnawing. They eat grass seeds and roots, as well as leaves. Grassland rodents include guinea pigs in the pampas, lemmings in the steppes, and deer mice, voles, and prairie dogs in the prairies. Many of these rodents also feed on grassland insects and spiders. This makes them secondary as well as primary **consumers.**

## What are prairie dogs?

Prairie dogs are not dogs at all. They are rodents that feed on prairie grasses and insects. They live in underground homes called burrows.

## Large grassland herbivores

There are also many large animals that feed on grasses. Some of these are birds. Ostriches in Africa, rheas in South America, and emus in Australia are all large, flightless birds that feed on grassland plants. In the African savanna there are large herds of antelopes, wildebeests, and zebras. In Australia kangaroos leap across grasslands in search of good grazing grounds. Bison and pronghorn deer graze on some parts of the prairies in the United States.

## Grassland secondary consumers

Many different kinds of animals feed on the grassland **herbivores.** Insects such as termites are eaten by anteaters and aardvarks. Lizards and snakes also eat termites when they leave the nest to find food. Snakes slither underground to eat burrowing herbivores such as prairie dogs. Falcons, owls, and hawks fly above grasslands to hunt **rodents.**

Some grassland **carnivores** such as lions and hyenas hunt in teams. They work together to bring down big herbivores such as wildebeests. After the carnivores have eaten, vultures, which are **scavengers,** circle the air searching for the remains of the dead animal to feast on.

## Prairie food web

This is a food web from a prairie **habitat.** It is made up of many separate food chains.

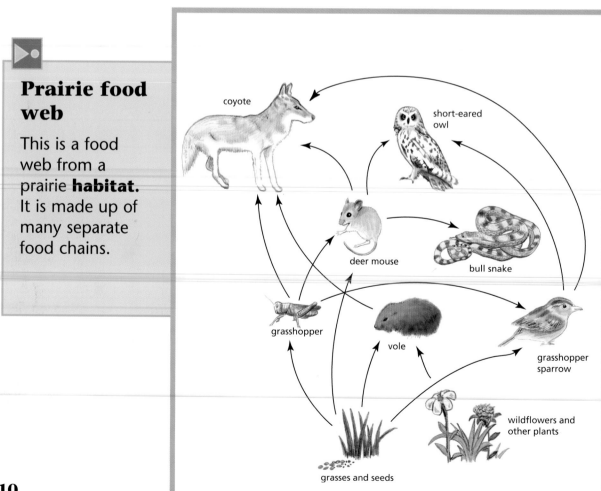

coyote

short-eared owl

deer mouse

bull snake

grasshopper

vole

grasshopper sparrow

wildflowers and other plants

grasses and seeds

# Who Eats Whom in Oceans, Rivers, and Lakes?

The oceans of the world cover more than three quarters of Earth's surface. They are full of life. However, few plants live in open oceans. This is because plants need sunlight for **photosynthesis,** and in the deep waters of the world's oceans there is very little sunlight. So what are the **producers** in an ocean food web?

## Ocean producers

The surface waters of the ocean look clear and empty, but they are actually packed with **plankton.** Plankton is the name given to the collection of microscopic **organisms** floating in the oceans. It is mostly made up of **algae** and microscopic animals. The algae in plankton are the producers in all ocean food webs. The billions of producers in plankton carry out 40 percent of all the photosynthesis that happens on Earth. This picture shows **diatoms,** a kind of alga.

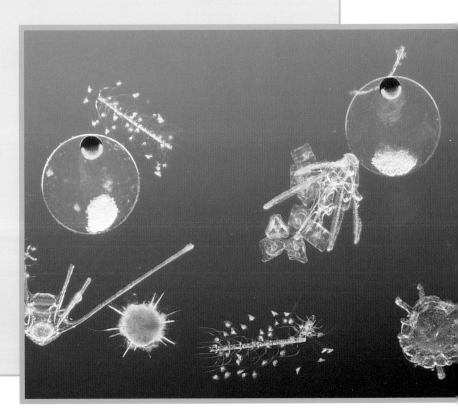

### Primary consumers

The smallest ocean **consumers** live within **plankton.** They include small, shrimplike animals called copepods. Plankton also includes the **larvae** of animals such as crabs and jellyfish. These consumers are **herbivores** that feed on the microscopic plants in plankton.

### Secondary consumers

Slightly larger **carnivores** such as fish and **krill** eat plankton. In turn, even larger animals such as fish and squid eat them. Seabirds, large fish such as tuna, and **mammals** such as sea lions and dolphins eat squid and other fish. The top **predators** in the world's oceans are great white sharks and killer whales.

## Filter-feeding giant

Whales are some of the largest animals on Earth. But many whales eat some of the smallest animals on Earth: krill. Most whales have rows of fringed plates called baleen. They push mouthfuls of water through their baleen and use a car-sized tongue to trap the krill. A whale can eat up to four tons of krill every day.

## Coastal food chains

Coastal waters are shallower than the open ocean. The land is covered and then exposed by rising and falling tides and crashing waves. Large **algae** called seaweeds grow attached to rocks in different depths of coastal waters. **Photosynthesis** happens in their fronds, or leaves.

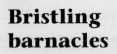

### Bristling barnacles

Barnacles live attached to coastal rocks. When the tide is in, they open their shells and wave their bristled legs to catch pieces of food.

Some **organisms** graze on algae. Mollusks are organisms that have soft bodies and hard protective shells. Some mollusks such as limpets move over algae-covered rocks and seaweed. They scrape off food with their rough tongues. Other mollusks such as dog whelks drill into these grazers' shells to eat them. Clams have two shells and live in sand. They come to the surface to feed on plankton and pieces of dead organisms. Birds such as oystercatchers feed on the mollusks.

### Producers in rivers and lakes

Rivers and most lakes contain freshwater, not saltwater like the oceans. The **producers** in deep lakes are **algae,** just like in the oceans. In rivers and in the shallow parts of lakes, there are larger water plants. Plants such as eelgrass grow in fast-moving water. They have long, thin leaves that do not drag and get damaged. In calm, shallow waters, plants such as water lilies are rooted at the bottom. They have large leaves that float on top of the water where they can catch sunlight.

### Freshwater feeders

The small grazers in rivers and lakes include small floating **organisms** called **protists,** as well as snails and tadpoles. Insects such as water fleas float on the water among the algae they feed on. Water striders slide across the surface of the water, catching food such as dead insects.

## Feeding in water

Large **herbivores** include moose, which paddle into rivers to feed on water plants. Manatees such as those shown here are large animals that hold their breath and swim slowly. They eat riverbed plants, often holding their food with their front flippers as they eat.

## Changing diet

Tadpoles graze on algae after they hatch from eggs. Later, they turn into **carnivores,** hunting organisms in the water at first. After becoming frogs, they hunt insects and slugs on land.

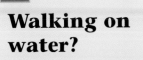

## Walking on water?

Jacanas have long toes that enable them to walk on water lily leaves. It looks as if they can walk on water. Jacanas are **omnivores.** They walk across floating water plants to find insects, other small animals, and plant seeds to eat.

## Freshwater secondary consumers

Some fish, such as trout, feed on insect **larvae** and drowned flies. Other fish feed on worms and snails from the riverbed. **Predators** such as pike hunt these fish. Birds such as herons hunt in shallow water, looking for fish to spear with their beaks.

In some rivers, crocodiles and alligators hunt underwater **prey** including fish and turtles. They sometimes hunt **mammals** such as deer that visit the rivers to drink.

## ACTIVITY: Draw an ocean food chain

Ocean food chains show how energy flows from small plants into **herbivores,** and finally into **carnivores.**

### EQUIPMENT

Large sheet of paper, pictures of a killer whale, sea lion, fish, **krill,** and a **diatom.** You can draw these from a book, cut them out of an old magazine, or print them out from a web page. Have an adult help you find the pictures.

### STEPS

1. Draw a horizontal line at the top of the paper to show the surface of the ocean.
2. Place the ocean **organisms** below the surface of the ocean. Put the **producers** at the bottom, the primary **consumers** in the middle, and the secondary consumers at the top.
3. Now draw arrows from each organism pointing to the organism that eats it. Use information from pages 11 through 13 to help you.

### EXPLANATION

This is one ocean food chain, but there are many more. A food chain shows the direction of the energy flow, but not the numbers of organisms. As you have learned, there would be more diatoms than killer whales in an ocean.

# What Are Food Webs Like in Dry Places?

The driest areas of the world are deserts and tundras. The deserts of the world are extremely hot and have very little rainfall. The land is rocky or covered in sand. A tundra is an area where water is frozen into ice and snow for most of the year, creating a dry **habitat.**

## Desert producers

The plants at the start of desert food chains and webs have different ways of getting the water they need to survive. Some have roots that spread far to catch any available rainfall or dew that seeps into the ground. Other plants such as cacti store water inside their fleshy stems. Many desert plants are **annuals** that grow from seeds and flower only for a short time after a rainstorm.

## Jumping jerboas!

Desert plants are food for many consumers, including this jerboa. Jerboas jump around on their long back legs to find seeds, roots, leaves, and insects to eat.

## Plant eaters in deserts

Desert plants provide food and water for the primary **consumers** that feed on them. Some insects feed on the **nectar** or leaves of the flowering plants. Many desert **herbivores** stay out of the heat and sun by hiding underground or under rocks. Naked mole rats live in burrows and tunnel through the soil feeding on roots and other underground plant parts. Kangaroo rats and other **rodents** eat cactus seeds. Some desert lizards eat fruits and leaves.

## Secondary consumers in the desert

Scorpions eat spiders and some small lizards. Desert lizards eat insects, moths, or smaller lizards. Like many desert animals, golden moles live in burrows to escape the heat of the Sun. They emerge to feed if they feel the movement of beetles, snakes, and lizards on the surface. Some snakes, like the sidewinder, eat small rodents such as the kangaroo rat. Meerkats are secondary consumers and primary consumers. They feed on scorpions (as shown here), insects, and the roots of many desert plants.

## Tundra plants

The tundra has short summers, but for most of the year the land is covered in snow or ice. In the tundra mosses grow in cushion shapes that trap warmth and water. The arctic dwarf willow grows low to the ground to stay out of the way of cold winds. Some flowering tundra plants survive underground as seeds in the winter. They grow leaves and flowers during the short summer.

## Tundra herbivores

Insects feed on the leaves of tundra plants. For example, in the Antarctic small insects called springtails eat dead moss. In summer, butterflies and bees feed on flower nectar. Some small **mammals** feed on plants, too. Lemmings live in tunnels beneath the Arctic snow. They eat roots and mosses. Arctic hares eat plants such as the arctic dwarf willow. Large tundra grazers include musk oxen that roam in search of plants to eat. Reindeer scrape the snow with their hooves and antlers to find plants to eat.

## Camouflage

Many tundra animals including arctic foxes and snowy owls (seen here) have white fur or feathers. This is a kind of **camouflage.** The light colors hide them from other animals they are hunting, or from animals that are hunting them.

**19**

# A tundra food web

Only a few **species** of plants and animals live in tundra habitats. That is why tundra food chains and webs like this one are so short.

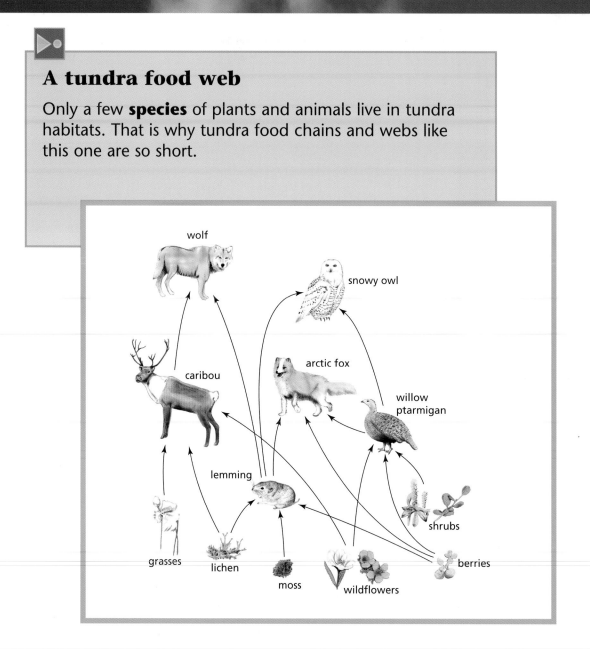

## Tundra secondary consumers

Arctic foxes and birds such as snowy owls and golden eagles eat lemmings and arctic hares. Wolves are too small to bring down large **prey** on their own. But together in packs, wolves can hunt musk oxen and caribou.

# Who Eats Whom in Forests?

The forests and woodlands of the world are dominated by very obvious **producers:** trees. These green plants have tall, woody stems that raise their leaves high into the air to catch sunlight for **photosynthesis.** Trees supply a wide range of **habitats** for all kinds of living things.

Many forests in **temperate** areas with warm summers and cold winters contain deciduous trees. Deciduous trees drop all of their leaves in the fall. They survive winter on sugars stored in their trunks. The leaves that these trees have dropped provide food for insect **larvae,** which are then eaten by birds. Many insects live and feed under tree bark and are eaten by birds such as woodpeckers.

## Squirrel treasures

Squirrels bury acorns in the soil to give them a store of food for the winter. They require a lot of energy to leap from tree to tree.

## From primary to secondary consumer

In temperate forests, other primary **consumers** include mammals such as deer, beavers, and porcupines that eat bark and branches. Caribou,

such as the one pictured here, find shelter among woodland trees and come out to graze on grass, young trees, and shrubs. Secondary consumers include omnivores such as badgers and bears, which eat anything from fruit, honey, and nuts to small mammals and eggs. Woodland carnivores include wolves and foxes, which use their sharp teeth to trap **prey.** Owls drop silently from the sky to catch small animals with their claws.

## A coniferous forest food chain

In **temperate** areas many forests contain conifers such as pine trees. The leaves and seeds of pine trees may be eaten by voles, which look like mice. Voles can be eaten by northern goshawks, gray owls, or even by the large, catlike lynx.

## Tropical forests

The tops of trees in a **tropical** forest form a high layer, or canopy, that is thick with leaves, fruits, and flowers. Primary consumers here include sloths and large-nosed proboscis monkeys that eat leaves. Fruit bats fly between trees in search of ripe fruit.

Secondary consumers in tropical forests include **omnivores** such as chimpanzees, which eat a range of food from fruit to very small antelopes on occasion. **Carnivores** include enormous spiders and centipedes that can kill birds and even **mammals.** Snakes climb trees to eat tree frogs, and eagles hunt monkeys. Big cats such as jaguars roam the forest floor in search of wild pigs, deer, and monkeys.

### Tropical treats

The agouti is a **rodent** with long legs that eats the fruits and nuts that drop to the ground. Its large, sharp front teeth are strong enough to bite through tough shells to reach the nuts inside.

## Decomposers

On the ground of all woodlands and forests is a layer of leaf litter made up of fallen leaves, branches, and dead animals. **Bacteria** and **fungi** are the **organisms** that **decompose** leaf litter. As they release **nutrients** to feed themselves, they also release nutrients that are used by trees and other plants. Fungi grow networks of tiny threads under the surface of the ground that look like cotton fibers. The parts of fungi you can see, such as mushrooms, are used for **reproduction.**

Mites, worms, and slugs eat fungi. Wood lice and millipedes also eat the decomposing leaf litter. Beetle **larvae** often eat harder rotting wood. These **herbivores** are hunted by secondary **consumers** such as spiders, centipedes, shrews, and salamanders.

## Forest food chains

This diagram shows how food chains combine into a food web in **temperate** forests.

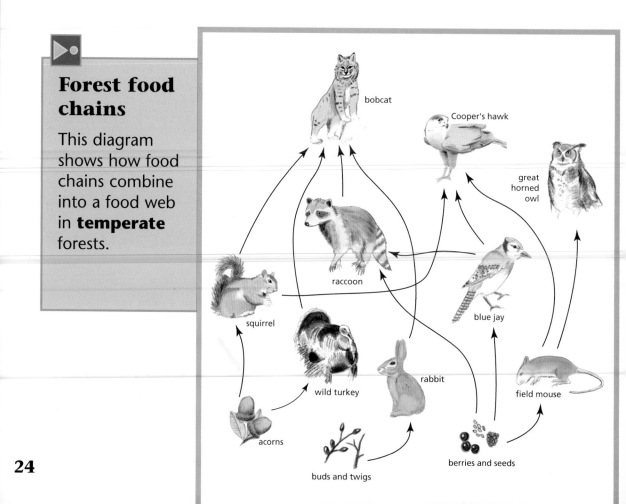

bobcat

Cooper's hawk

great horned owl

raccoon

blue jay

squirrel

wild turkey

rabbit

field mouse

acorns

buds and twigs

berries and seeds

# What are Food Webs Like in Towns and Cities?

You might think that it would be hard to find food chains and webs in towns and cities. In fact, many animals live in **habitats** such as parks and yards. Some animals eat the same food as they would in their natural habitats. Other animals feed on people's garbage.

## Parks and yards

Animals that form food chains in parks and yards usually eat the same kinds of food as they would in the wild. The plants and trees in yards and parks attract butterflies, bees, and other insects that feed on **nectar** and **pollen.** Worms live under lawns, and birds eat them. Slugs and snails graze on plants. Toads and birds eat the snails and slugs. Some of the main **predators** are pet cats, which hunt birds and small **mammals** such as mice.

### Bird food

Many birds have found ways to live in cities and towns. They even find places to live in buildings, such as these English robins in an old tool shed. However, many birds still eat the same kinds of food that they would eat in natural areas.

## Houses and streets

When people take over natural **habitats,** some of the animals are forced to eat food that is very different from what they would eat in the wild. Indoors, houseflies eat human food. Cockroaches eat all kinds of things including food scraps and even soap! Rats and mice chew holes in cupboards and packages to get at the food in people's homes. On the street, foxes, raccoons (shown here), and in some areas even bears search for food in garbage cans. Gulls and pigeons eat scraps from the streets and from **landfills.**

### Night feeders

Many animals living in towns and cities feed at night, when few people are around. In farm towns, barn owls swoop down to feed on small animals such as mice. Bats fly near street lamps to catch insects in the air.

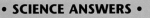
## ACTIVITY: Draw human food chains

Humans are part of food chains, too. Humans get energy from food just like other animals. Humans' food comes from plants or from animals that have eaten plants.

### EQUIPMENT
Large sheet of paper; pictures of foods, drinks, animals such as cows and chickens, plants such as wheat and grass, and a photograph of yourself. You can draw these from a book, cut them out of an old magazine, or print them out from a web page. Have an adult help you find the pictures.

### STEPS
1. Choose some of the meals you like to eat and figure out where they came from. For example, bread is made from wheat. Hamburgers come from cows that eat grass.
2. Put the photo of yourself at the top of the paper. Place the **producers** at the bottom and the **consumers** in the middle.
3. Draw arrows pointing to you from each food that you eat and from the animal or plant that it came from.

### EXPLANATION
The food chains you have made show the direction of energy flow from primary producers to you. You are the last link in these food chains because humans do not have any successful **predators.**

## John Muir (1838-1914)

John Muir (shown here) was a Scottish explorer in the United States and other parts of the world. His writings were unusual at that time because he understood that people are part of the web of nature. Muir worked to protect wild places as national parks for all to enjoy. He wrote, "When we try to pick out anything by itself, we find it hitched to everything else in the Universe."

## Rachel Carson (1907-1964)

Rachel Carson was a scientist and writer. She studied the effects of using chemicals to kill disease-carrying insects such as mosquitoes. In her book *Silent Spring,* she showed that these chemicals affected many other creatures, from harmless insects to people. She also revealed that killing these insects has a major effect on food chains since they provide food for birds and other animals. Her work helped create laws to make sure that chemicals are safe before they are used in wild **habitats.**

# Amazing Facts

- More than half of the world's estimated ten million **species** of plants and animals live in tropical forests.

- A dead leaf takes six weeks to decay completely in leaf litter.

- There are as many as four million **bacteria** in each ton of soil.

- Mako sharks can swim at almost 60 miles (97 kilometers) per hour. Cheetahs (pictured below) can run at nearly 45 miles (72 kilometers) per hour. Peregrine falcons can fly at over 185 miles (300 kilometers) per hour. These are some of the fastest **predators** in the world.

- In a city, some bats can catch and eat up to 3,000 insects in one night.

- The largest ocean predator is the sperm whale, which measures 55 feet (17 meters) in length.

 # Glossary

**alga** (more than one are algae)   single-celled organism that makes its own food like a plant

**annual**   plant that grows from a seed and reproduces in one growing season

**bacterium** (more than one are bacteria)   common single-celled organism with no nucleus

**camouflage**   pattern or color that matches an animal's habitat so that it cannot be seen easily

**carbon dioxide**   gas found in small amounts in air. Plants use it for photosynthesis and animals breathe it out.

**carnivore**   animal that eats other animals

**consumer**   living thing that eats other living things

**decompose**   break down a dead organism into nutrients

**diatom**   marine organism with two hard shells that form a box around its body

**fungus** (more than one are fungi)   type of living thing that is not an animal or a plant. Fungi include mushrooms, molds, yeasts, and toadstools.

**krill**   small, shrimplike animal

**habitat**   natural home of a group of plants or animals

**herbivore**   animal that eats plants

**landfill**   place where garbage is taken

**larva** (more than one are larvae)   young that looks very different from its parents and must undergo changes before it becomes an adult

**mammal**   kind of animal that feeds its babies milk from its own body and has some hair

**nectar**   sugary liquid that plants make in their flowers to attract insects and birds

**nutrient**   chemical that plants and animals need in order to live

**omnivore**   organism that eats both plants and animals

**organism**   living thing

**photosynthesis**   process by which plants make their own food using water, carbon dioxide, and energy from sunlight

**plankton**   group of microscopic organisms that live in the surface waters of the oceans

**pollen**   small, dustlike particle that contains male sex cells

**predator**   animal that hunts and catches other animals

**prey**   animal that is caught and eaten by another animal

**producer**   living thing that makes its own food

**protist**   microscopic organism with a nucleus

**reproduction**   when a living thing produces young like itself

**rodent**   kind of mammal with large teeth

**savanna**   kind of grassland with dry and rainy seasons that has some trees and bushes

**scavenger**   animal that eats dead organisms

**species**   group of organisms that have similar characteristics

**temperate**   not too hot or too cold

**tropical**   having hot weather throughout the year

# More Books to Read

Knight, Tim. *Fantastic Feeders*. Chicago: Heinemann Library, 2003.

McGinty, Alice B. *Decomposers in the Food Chain*. New York: Rosen Publishing, 2002.

Nadeau, Isaac. *Food Chains in a Tide Pool Habitat*. New York: Rosen Publishing, 2002.

# Index